Follow the Star

Book and Lyrics by
WALLY K. DALY

Music by
JIM PARKER

International Music Publications Limited
Griffin House 161 Hammersmith Road London W6 8BS England

FOLLOW THE STAR

CHARACTERS IN ORDER OF APPEARANCE

OLLY	Baritone
GABBY	Tenor
ANGY	Contralto
JELLY	Soprano
LOFTY	Baritone
ANGEL CHICAGO	Tenor
HEROD	High Baritone
MARY	Contralto
JOSEPH	Baritone
1ST WISE MAN	Tenor
2ND WISE MAN	Baritone
3RD WISE MAN	Baritone
OXY	Non-singing
ASSY	
VILLAGERS	Chorus
SHEPHERDS	
OTHER ANGELS	
SOLDIERS	
ZAC	

MUSICAL ITEMS

ACT I

1.	Overture	
2.	"Kindly Sit Down At Your Places"	OLLY and CHORUS
3.	"Every Time You're Good You Grow A Bit"	GABBY and CHORUS
3a.	"Mary, Mary"	VOICES OFF-STAGE
4.	"I've Always Wanted a Baby"	MARY, JOSEPH, ANGY, JELLY and LOFTY
5.	"I'm Going To Be a Star"	GABBY and CHORUS
5a.	Magic Bell Music	ORCHESTRA
6.	"Nice Boys And Girls"	HEROD
7.	"Tension"	CHICAGO, HEROD, OLLY and CHORUS
8.	"Nice Boys And Girls" (*Reprise*)	HEROD
8a.	Magic Sounds	ORCHESTRA
9.	"Follow The Star"	THREE KINGS, GABBY and CHORUS (*Off-stage*)
10.	"Home"	MARY, JOSEPH and CHORUS
11.	"We Won't Let The Baby Die"	CHICAGO, HEROD, KINGS and CHORUS

ACT II

12.	Entr'acte	ORCHESTRA
13.	"Careful, Carefree or Careless"	ANGEL CHICAGO
14.	"There Is No Room"	ANGY, JELLY, LOFTY and CHORUS (*Off-stage*)
15.	Dance	OXY and ASSY
15a.	To Open Shepherds' Scene	ORCHESTRA
16.	"A Baby's Been Born" (*Angels' Song*)	ANGY, JELLY, LOFTY and CHORUS
17.	"We'll Always Love Him"	MARY, JOSEPH and CHORUS (*Off-stage*)
18.	"A Baby's Been Born" (*Reprise*)	CHORUS (*with* ANGY, JELLY *and* LOFTY)
19.	"Follow The Star" (*Reprise*)	THREE WISE MEN
20.	"We All Love You. Yes We Do"	OLLY and ALL
21.	"Kindly Sit Down" (*Reprise*)	OLLY
22.	"Clap Your Hands And Be Cheery"	OLLY and COMPANY
23.	"Clap Your Hands"—Bows	COMPANY

Music No. 1. Overture

ACT I

OLLY Stop! Hello all of you. (*Wait for reply.*)

Hello! Lovely! I'm Olly. I'm the "Boss" up here.

Music No. 2. "*KINDLY SIT DOWN AT YOUR PLACES*" (OLLY and ALL).

(*Before the house lights are fully out.*)

OLLY (*Sings*)
Kindly sit down at your places
Wipe the ice-cream off your faces.
Boys don't pinch the girls in front,
And girls don't pinch the boys behind.

Lads don't tease your little brother,
Do not aggravate your mother.
Do not stand upon the seat
And then jump down on daddy's feet.

Don't loudly chew your crisps and crunchies,
Do not play a game of punchies,
Little ladies do not wriggle
Even though you've got a tickle.

(*Spoken*) Come on Angels! These slides need dusting.

(*Sung*)
Soon I'm going to start the story,
I hope you're going to love the play.
As soon as you're quiet, I'll have the lights out
And then if you're good, I'll go away.

Our play starts up in heaven,
You'll see the angels gathered there.
We're going to tell how Christmas started,
And I bet you soon wish that you were there.

You can cheer your fav'rite angel,
You can boo the baddies too.
I don't even mind if you talk together
But don't fall asleep whatever you do

'Cos then you'd miss bits of the story,
And when you woke it'd be time to go,
And when your friends said
You would have to say "I don't know!"

> I've done my bit and got you quiet.
> You're all being good so now I'll go.
> All that's left for me to say is————
>
> (*Spoken*) Enjoy yourselves!

OLLY   Who's on duty today?

GABBY   I am.

OLLY   Who are you?

GABBY   I'm Gabriel. My friends call me Gabby.

OLLY   You're not a very big angel are you?

GABBY   Well you've got to start little haven't you. I mean, I haven't done any jobs yet. You know as well as I do that I've got to do jobs before I can get bigger—haven't I?

OLLY   Well. I've got a job for you today. Give you a start.

GABBY   You haven't?

OLLY   I have.

GABBY   A job for me. For me. Little Gabriel. I've never had a job before. Yahoo! I've got a job!

ANGELS   Well done! Great Gabby! etc.

OLLY   Come back here. It's a very important job, so you make sure you do it right. Alright?

GABBY   Right. You must tell me what I've got to do.

OLLY   Well. You've got to go to the city of Nazareth. Find a lady called Mary, and tell her she's going to have a baby.

GABBY   Aw. A baby.

OLLY   Do you think you can manage that?

GABBY   Yes. I can do that. Go to the city of Nazareth. Find a lady called Mary. Tell her she's going to have a baby. Yes. I can do that.

OLLY   Very good. I'll leave it to you. Hey! You three.

LOFTY   Us?

OLLY	Yes. Which ones are you?
ANGY	I'm Angy.
LOFTY	I'm Lofty.
JELLY	I'm Jelly.
OLLY	Well. Help the others tidy up, and when you're finished, come and see me in the office. Right?
ANGY **JELLY** **LOFTY**	(*Eager*) Right!
OLLY	I might have a job for you too.

(OLLY *exits.*)

(ANGELS *start removing clouds etc.* GABBY *moves downstage.*)

GABBY (*to Audience*) I've got a job! My very first job. All these years I've been up here and now I've finally got a job. You see, there're so many of us up here, and we've got to share the work out between us. And you only get a turn every few hundred years. And when it's your turn, if there's no job for you to do, you've had it. You go back to the end of the queue and start waiting all over again. Well, today I've got a job. I'm going to tell a lady called—what was her name again? Oh, that's right, Mary. I'm going to tell Mary she's going to have a baby. What a nice job. I'd better practise. (*Clears throat*) "Excuse me. You're going to have a baby." No. I'll have to do it a bit better than that. Perhaps a voice like thunder. (*Voice like thunder*) "You're going to have a baby!!" No. I mustn't frighten her must I. Oh how lovely—a job—my very first job. (*To himself. Practising*) *You're* going to have a baby. You're *going* to have a baby. You're going to have a *baby*. (*To Audience*) I must do it well. I might grow a bit if I do it really well. See, it's alright for you lot, if you're good you get fuller and fuller of goodness. But we angels get taller and taller and taller. So if you're a small angel everybody knows you haven't done many jobs don't they? So you've got to do lots of good jobs. 'Cos "Every time you're good, you grow a bit." I'll get the angels to help explain. Hey fellas!

(*Everyone except* OLLY *and* HEROD *sing song.* CHICAGO *in at end.*)
Music No. 3. "*EVERY TIME YOU'RE GOOD YOU GROW A BIT*" (GABBY *and* CHORUS).

GABBY	Help old ladies across the street, On a crowded train why not give someone your seat. Try to be friendly to people you meet, 'Cos every time you're good you grow a bit. Try to laugh when told a joke by your dad, Own up straight away when you're caught being bad. Try to cheer up somebody who's sad, 'Cos every time you're good you grow a bit.
GABBY and CHORUS	Every time you're good you grow a bit, Every time you're good it shows a bit, Every time you're good you grow a bit, You grow a little bit more.
GABBY	Whistle at ladies who are plain and fat, Try not to trip over your Granny's cat, Write a big welcome on the front mat, 'Cos every time you're good you grow a bit.
GABBY and CHORUS	Every time you're good you grow a bit
ANGY and LOFTY	(*Grow a bit*)
ALL	Every time you're good it shows a bit,
ANGY and LOFTY	(*Shows a bit*)
ALL	Every time you're good you grow a bit,
ANGY and LOFTY	(*Grow a bit*)
ALL	You grow a little bit more.
(ALL)	Remember this tune, yes remember this song, Hum it to yourself as you walk along And it will remind you not to do wrong, 'Cos every time you're good you grow a bit. (*Above sung in unison, change of key. Then repeat in harmony.*) Remember this tune, yes remember this song, Hum it to yourself as you walk along And it will remind you not to do wrong 'Cos every time you're good you grow a little bit more, more!
BASSES	Grow a bit,

TENORS	Grow a bit,
ALTOS	Grow a bit,
SOPRANOS	Grow a bit
ALL	More! A little bit More, more, more, grow a bit More, more, more, grow a bit More, more, more, more, Grow a little bit more!

(*Orchestra continue for exit.*)

(*Whole Company joins in. One strangely dressed* ANGEL *wearing a bowler hat, a short angel costume, and having red garters holding his socks up, tries to join in the dancing, but is always missed out by the others. All the* ANGELS *leave at the end of the song except this* ANGEL. *He stands alone centre stage. He takes a cigar from inside his bowler hat and lights it. Very sad, he walks downstage. Talks to Audience.*)

ANGEL CHICAGO   My name's Chicago. Angel Chicago. I'm King Herod's angel. The others don't like me very much. You may have noticed. It's because I'm Herod's guardian angel. I can't help being King Herod's angel. I mean everybody's got a guardian angel haven't they. Good people, and bad people. It's not my fault I'm guardian angel to the worst, worst worst man there is—is it. King Herod. A real baddy. It's not my fault—I just do my job. Stand at his shoulder all day long whispering. "Do good. Don't be bad. Do good. Don't be bad." But does it do any good—naw. He just does bad all the time. I thought he might be deaf in one ear, so I changed sides, but it didn't make any difference, he just went on being bad. I think his badness is starting to rub off on me. I keep making burn holes in all the clouds with my ash, making Olly angry, and that's bad. Here—that Herod—he don't half give me a bad time. I hope you lot don't give your guardian angels a bad time. Do you? Do you give your guardian angel a bad time? No? How about you; do you give your guardian angel a bad time? Yes? No? (*Ad libbed*) Alright! We are going to have a little examination. Hands up those of you here who are really really good. (*Ad libbed*) Right, hands down. Hands up, those of you who are really really bad. (*Ad libbed*) Right hands down. Hands up all those of you who are a bit naughty sometimes. Come on own up—now be honest. Who's a little bit naughty sometimes? Anyway—you've got to be a little bit naughty sometimes, haven't you? Even I'm a little bit naughty sometimes. Still—no matter how naughty you were you couldn't be as bad as Herod. Herod's horrid. Terrible.

HEROD	(*shouting off-stage*) Where's my bag of royal jelly babies?
ANGEL CHICAGO	That's him coming now. But don't worry too much. I will look after you. You see, as I'm his guardian angel he can't see me. But he can see you lot, so if he gets really bad and starts leaping off into the audience like this, (*Ad lib* "She didn't flinch!" *etc*) do not fear. We'll blow him off the stage and down into one of the exit holes. Right? When I go like that, I want you to blow, and when I go like that, I want you to stop. Let's have a little practise before he comes on. Are you ready? Right, 1, 2, 3 (*Audience blows. Pause.*) Did you do it?... Rubbish! We'll do it again and I want you to blow a hundred times harder. Right? 1, 2, 3 (*Audience blows. Pause.*) The kids were good—but the grown ups were terrible. Kids, will you help me out this time?... We're going to do it again and if there's a grown up sitting next to you who's not blowing, will you stand up on your seat, point at him and say, "He's not blowing!" Will you do that? Right, are you ready, 1, 2, 3 (*Audience blows*) Fantastic!

(HEROD *enters.*)

HEROD	Stand aside for the Royal Me! King Herod—the Wonderful. King Herod the Beautiful. King Herod the Bountiful. The most Grandiose and Gorgeous. King of Kings. Star of Stars. Eighth wonder of the world. What am I saying? Eighth wonder? First wonder of the world. I King Herod. Regal but Merciful. No jewelled crown could shine as bright as I. But still I remain— humble.
CHICAGO	We'd noticed that—hadn't we.

HEROD	(*Sniffs*) What's that funny smell? (*Smells something strange, but carries on regardless.*) Oh never mind. King Herod. King of the stars. And star of the Kings. Magnificent! Magnetic! Magnanimous! Majestical!
	    Who's the biggest, who's the best,
	    Who can always beat the rest—
	    My Royal High Herodness!

CHICAGO	Your Royal High Horridness!
HEROD	Three cheers for King Herod. (HEROD *gives three quick Hip Hip Hoorays!*) Three more for luck. (*Gives three more Hip Hip Hoorays.*) We; Believe—that I am marvellous and We; are right.
CHICAGO	Oh stop showing off, Herod! You know what happens when you start showing off. (HEROD *sniffs.*)

HEROD	What's that funny smell? (*Sniffs again*) I think it's... Oh no!... Oh yes... it's (*Looks at audience*) Yak! Boys and girls! Look at them all! Agh! Nasty. Oh how I hate nice boys and girls. Yak!
CHICAGO	(*Follows him around*) Stop it Herod! Be good!
HEROD	Oh! Look at that one. He's been washed. He's all clean. How horrible.
CHICAGO	He's lovely. Leave him alone. Don't be bad!
HEROD	Look! there's one with clean shoes. Yak!
CHICAGO	Be good. Don't be bad.
HEROD	Look! Look! Over there, a girl with a new frock. And there's another one. Yak! You're all horribly nice! I can't stand it any more. Let me out of here.
CHICAGO	It's no good, I can't stop him; Blow. We'll have to blow him down that exit hole.
HEROD	Yak! Yak! Yak! Nasty little Creepies!
CHICAGO	Go on! Keep on blowing! Well done! (*Etc.*) Be good Herod, don't be bad.
	Music No. 3a. "*MARY, MARY*" (*Voice off-stage.*)
	(*Thunder and lightning in blackout.*)
TWO SOPRANOS	MARY! MARY! MARY?
	(*Spotlight on bed that has arrived stage right.* MARY *sits up in bed with a start.*)
MARY	Who's that! Who's there? (*Spotlight on* ANGEL GABRIEL *who is up high. Stage left.*)
GABBY	Don't be frightened, Mary—it's only me. (GABRIEL *comes down.*)
MARY	Who are you?
GABBY	Oh. I'm Gabby... er... Angel Gabriel. I've got some lovely news for you.
MARY	You frightened the life out of me. What are you doing in my bedroom at this time of night?

GABBY I'm on a job. I've come to give you some news. I've got a message for you from Heaven.

MARY What is it?

GABBY You'll never guess. You're going to have a baby.

MARY I'm not.

GABBY You are. A little baby. That's what my message is.

MARY I'm not!

GABBY You are! (*To Audience*) Isn't she? That's what my message is. You're going to have a baby.

MARY Oh a baby—how lovely. I've always wanted a baby since I was a girl. What sort is it going to be?

GABBY Pardon?

MARY What sort is it going to be?

GABBY What do you mean?

MARY What sort is it going to be. A boy or a girl.

GABBY Er. I don't know, I didn't ask. I was only told to say you were going to have a baby. That's all. Hang on. (*To Audience*) Do you know if it's going to be a boy or a girl? Pardon? Oh. They say it's going to be a boy.

MARY A boy. I've always wanted a baby. Joseph will be pleased.

GABBY Who's that?

MARY Who's what?

GABBY Joseph. Who's that?

MARY Joseph, my betrothed. I'll call him and tell him. Joseph! Joseph!!

GABBY Shouldn't you sit down and take it easy Mary. You're going to have a baby. You've got to go careful now you know.

MARY Oh I'll be alright—Joseph!!!

(JOSEPH *enters.*)

JOSEPH	What is it Mary?
MARY	You'll never guess what.
JOSEPH	What?
MARY	I'm going to have a baby.
JOSEPH	What!
MARY	This angel's just told me.
JOSEPH	What angel Mary?
MARY	This one. Here.
GABBY	I should explain Mary—you can see me but he can't.
MARY	Why not?
GABBY	Well I was sent to give a message to you. Not to anybody else. Just you.
JOSEPH	Who are you talking to Mary?
MARY	Hang on a sec Joseph. Do you mean Joseph can't see you Gabby?
GABBY	That's it.
MARY	You realize it makes it very difficult for me. Joseph and I are betrothed. He's got to know I'm having a baby, now hasn't he? Can't you see you're making it very difficult for me.
GABBY	Well I was just told to tell you, you were having a baby—that's all my job is. Just to tell you. I don't know if I'm allowed to let anyone else see me. This is my first job. I don't want to mess it up. Hang on. (*To Audience*) Should I let Joseph see me as well? Pardon? Oh all right. I'll let him see me. Joseph!
JOSEPH	Agh! (JOSEPH *reacts at seeing* GABBY)
GABBY	It's alright it's only me. Gabby. Angel Gabriel. He can see me now Mary. It's all right Joseph. Don't be frightened. I've just been talking to Mary. She's going to have a baby and they all say it's going to be a girl. You what? Oh sorry, yes a boy. A boy. Isn't that nice? So now you both know I'll be off. Tara Mary. Tara Joseph. (*To Audience*) Do I look any bigger? Oh well. Never mind. Perhaps later. (GABRIEL *exits and pops back again*) I did that very well didn't I. "You're going to have a baby." (*Exits*)

MARY We're going to have a baby Joseph. A little boy.

JOSEPH A baby boy. How lovely. I've always wanted a baby.

MARY So have I. Ever since I was a girl.

Music No. 4. *"I'VE ALWAYS WANTED A BABY"* (MARY, JOSEPH, ANGY, JELLY *and* LOFTY).

MARY (*sings*)
I've always wanted a baby,
Since I was very small,
I've always wanted a baby,
Since I was just this tall.

I played with my dolls,
Pretended they were real,
But with a real baby,
What a difference you feel.

I've always wanted a baby
Since I was very small.

JOSEPH
I've always wanted a baby,
'specially a baby boy.
Now you're having a baby,
I am full of joy.

	ANGY, JELLY and LOFTY
I'll teach him to box,	Ah
I'll teach him to run,	Ah
I'll teach him to swim,	Ah
Yes, We'll have lots of fun.	Ah

MARY and JOSEPH
I've always wanted a baby,
'specially a baby boy.

We are having a baby,
A little baby boy.
Now we know we're having a baby,
There's so much more to enjoy.

	ANGY, JELLY and LOFTY
We can	Ah
Walk in the sun, our	Ah
Hearts full of pride	Ah
Now that the angel has	Ah
Told us of the baby inside.	Ah

MARY and JOSEPH (Cont'd.)	We've Always wanted a baby, 'specially A baby Boy!	Ah Ah Ah

(*Orchestra continues under dialogue*)

JOSEPH Hey. Mary. I've just thought of something.

MARY What Joseph.

JOSEPH Well. We haven't thought of a name for him yet.

MARY Oh there's no rush. It's ages before I'll have him.

JOSEPH I know, but as we know it's going to be a boy, it would be nice to think of him—by name. You know, baby something, instead of just baby. What shall we call him Mary?

MARY Oh there's so many lovely boys names aren't there. Frederick, Tommy . . . What do you think we should call him Joseph?

JOSEPH How about—Dominic; or Steven perhaps.

MARY I know—Joshua; or Julian or Jack (*Joseph shakes his head.*)—what then?

JOSEPH I don't know. Now, what shall we call him?
(*Play it by ear until.*)
I seem to sense; the name Jesus.

MARY Jesus?

JOSEPH Baby Jesus—yes. That's lovely.

MARY Oh yes. Let's call him Jesus.

(*Song continues*)

MARY and JOSEPH We are having a baby,
A little baby boy.
Now we know we're having a baby,
There's so much more to enjoy.

		ANGY, JELLY and LOFTY
MARY and JOSEPH (Cont'd.)	We can Walk in the sun, our Hearts full of pride Now that the angel has Told us of the Baby inside.	Ah Ah Ah Ah Ah
	We've Always wanted a baby,	Ah Do doop, doop
	We've Always wanted a baby, we've Always wanted a baby,	Doop, doop a doop Ah Ah
	Especially A baby boy!	— — A baby boy!

(*Orchestra continues for exit of* JOSEPH *and* MARY)

(*At the end of song* MARY *and* JOSEPH *exit.* GABBY *enters stage left.*)

GABBY   Olly. Olly! It's me Gabby. I'm back. Olly! Anyone at home?

(OLLY *arrives.*)

Hello Olly. I'm back. I did very well. (*To Audience*) Didn't I? (*Voice like thunder*) "You're going to have a baby," I was lovely.

OLLY   You don't look any taller.

GABBY   Well. Perhaps it hasn't worked yet. I haven't been back long. I was very good.

OLLY   It should have worked by now. Did you do the job properly?

GABBY   Yes. Of course I did. No messing about. "You're going to have a baby." She was very pleased. I did *exactly* what you said. Exactly.

OLLY   Exactly?

GABBY   Exactly.

(*Long pause as* OLLY *stares at him and* GABBY *fights with his conscience.*)

And a tiny bit more. Nothing very much.

OLLY   Yeeess. Go on.

GABBY	Well. We thought, this lot and I, We thought That as Joseph, Mary's betrothed, was there as well, and couldn't see me, and kept saying, "Who are you talking to Mary?" We thought, this lot and I. That it would be nice, we thought, if he could—see me as well, you see.
OLLY	Oh no! (*Little bit of thunder and lightning*) How could you do such a thing.
GABBY	It was *us* actually. Us. Me and them.
OLLY	To go beyond your instructions is not really good Gabriel. I'm afraid that's the reason you aren't any taller. And now you have to go back to the end of the queue, and start waiting all over again. Oh—you silly little angel.
GABBY	Oh Olly. I wasn't being really bad. Honest. Can't you give me another chance.
OLLY	No. I'm sorry. That's impossible.
GABBY	Go on Olly. Go on, give me another chance.
OLLY	Well . . . No, I'm sorry.
GABBY	(*to Audience*) Come on you lot, ask him to give me another chance. It's as much your fault as mine. It was you who told me to let Joseph see me. Ask him to give me another chance. (*Play it by ear until.*)
OLLY	Oh all right. But this is your very last chance.
GABBY	Oh thank you Olly. And thank you as well. Well Olly. What's my job. I'm ready.
OLLY	Now listen, very carefully. No slip-ups this time. And no additions. Right?
GABBY	Right. What is it? I'm ready.
OLLY	Well, very soon three wise men are going to find out about Mary's baby, and the fact that the baby's going to be a new King. Right?
GABBY	Right. I'm going to tell them. Right?
OLLY	Wrong. They're going to find out from old manuscripts and ancient books. Right?
GABBY	Right. I'm going to tell them which page to look on. Right?

OLLY	Wrong. Angy, Jelly and Lofty are looking after that. Now the three wise men are going to follow a star, to the place where the baby's going to be born. Right?
GABBY	Right. And I'm going to be there to meet them at the other end. Right?
OLLY	Wrong. You're going to be the star. The star they follow. (*Slowly* GABBY's *face illuminates with pleasure at the thought. His eyes glaze.*)

OLLY	Do you understand. You're going to be the star the three wise men follow.
	   (GABBY *nods his head.*)
	
	All the way from their lands to Bethlehem.
	   (GABBY *nods his head.*)
	
	Through deserts and mountains.
	   (GABBY *nods his head.*)
	
	Do you think you can do it?
	   (GABBY *nods his head.*)
	
	It's not a five minute job, it'll take five or six months you know.
	   (GABBY *nods.*)
	
	Well. I'll leave it to you then. Enjoy yourself up there.
	   (OLLY *exits.*)

GABBY	(*still transfixed with pleasure*) A star. I'm going to be a star. Music No. 5. "*I'M GOING TO BE A STAR*" (GABBY *and* ALL *except* OLLY, HEROD *and* CHICAGO).
GABBY	(*Spoken, sotto voce*) A star! A star! I'm going to be a star! (*Sings*) A star! A star! I'm going to be a star! A star! A star! I'm gonna be a star. A star! A star! I'm gonna be a star!

GABBY (*Sings*) (**Cont'd.**)

I used to dream of it,
My dream's come true.
My name's in lights,
I'm applauded by you.

This little kid,
He has now made good.
I'll be a star
And I think I should

Say, thank you; and you,
And you, and you,
And you, and you,
And you!...

                CHORUS
                A star! A star!
                He's gonna be a star.
                A star, a star,
                He's gonna be a star!

ANGY (*shouted*) Hurrah!

GABBY (*sings*)

Only your cheers have put me where I am.	Ah
Without your support just another "Also ran".	Ah
The waiting was worth it, The effort was, too.	Ah
I've finally made it, my thanks to you....	Ah
A star,	
....	A star!
A star,	
....	A star!
I'm gonna be a star!	
A star,	He's gonna be a star,
A star,	A star!
	A star!
I'm gonna be a star!	
	He's gonna be a star,
	Going to be a star!

Thank you all, You've been so nice,	Ah
Your cheers and applause have been paradise,	Ah
I'll try to live up to it, I'll try to shine,	Ah
And I'll always remember you, Friends of mine	Ah
A star! A star! I'm gonna be a star!	Ah
A star, A star!	Ah
I'm going to be a star!	He's going to be a star!
I'm going to be a star! A star! A star!	He's going to be a star!

(BLACKOUT—HEROD *comes from the back of the auditorium followed by* CHICAGO.)

HEROD Lights! Lights give me some light! Oh I hate green—peppermint. (*Sings*) A star, a star, I've always been a star.
Ahh! Look! They're still here! Boys and girls. Yuk!

CHICAGO Be good Herod—you old rotter. Be good.

HEROD Look at them all. How I hate nice boys and girls. Horrid! Are there any nasty boys and girls here to be my friends?

CHICAGO No!

HEROD Are there any nasty boys and girls here?

CHICAGO NO!

HEROD Did I hear someone shout yes?

CHICAGO No!

HEROD Oh yes I did.

CHICAGO Oh no you didn't!

} Three times.

(OLLY *is by now watching from his level and as the shouting reaches a peak shouts.*)

HEROD Oh ye....

OLLY (*shouts above noise*) STOP!!!

(HEROD *and* CHICAGO *freeze in waxwork poses.*)

(*looks at* HEROD. *Looks at* CHICAGO. *Looks at audience. Speaks quietly*).
  Did I hear someone say Yes? No? Good. Now—what's going on? Hang on—one at a time. Right, you lot tell me. All right, all right, all right. I'll ask Angel Chicago. (*Clicks his finger.*)

Music No. 5a. "*MAGIC BELL MUSIC*" (ORCHESTRA)

(ANGEL CHICAGO *unfreezes and hops to the same level as* OLLY. *Wakes up.*)

CHICAGO (*still in preceding scene*) Oh no you didn't!

(*Realizes* OLLY's *there. Looks embarrassed*)

OLLY	All right, Chicago, we've had that bit. Now what's going on? I can't work for all the noise.
CHICAGO	It's not me, OLLY. It's rotten old Herod. He keeps shouting at them all the time—saying nasty things.
OLLY	Why?
CHICAGO	I don't know. He just does, that's all. All the time.
OLLY	Oh! And do they know why Herod shouts all the time?
CHICAGO	I don't know.
OLLY	Well, ask them.
CHICAGO	Do you know why Herod shouts at you all the time? Pardon? Oh, thank you. They said: (*indecipherable gibberish*) "Wadee wadee wadee wa".
OLLY	Well, let's find out from the man himself. (OLLY *flicks his fingers.* (*Music stops*) HEROD *comes awake with a start.* HEROD's *song.* OLLY *shushes the audience if there's any booing.*) Music No. 6. "*NICE BOYS AND GIRLS*" (HEROD)
HEROD (*sings*)	Nice boys and girls, I really hate them! Nice boys and girls make me mad. Nice boys and girls are gruesome! Give me children who are bad! Nice boys and girls are rubbish! Nice boys and girls are really yak! Nice boys and girls are horrific! Why not bring nasty children back?
(*Spoken*)	You're all scruffy and slimy and sloppy and stupid, Hideously odious, obnoxious as cupid. You're putrid and pongy and sickly as slugs, As plaguish as ants and as pleasant as bugs. You're all grisly and ghastly and glaringly gruesome, Putrescent, repellent, repulsively pukesome. Musty and monstrous and mouldy as mice, You're boringly, yawningly, horribly nice!
(*Sings*)	Nice boys and girls are monstrosities, Though a small one makes a tasty snack!

HEROD (*Spoken*) (*Cont'd.*)   Yum, yum, yum!

(*Sings*)   Nice boys and girls are grotesqueries.
Why not bring nasty children back!

(*Spoken*)   Dance!

(*Dance.*)

(*Sings*)   Nice boys and girls are disastrous,
Nice boys and girls are yuk yuk yak!
Nice boys and girls are grotesqueries!
Why not, why not, why not,
Why not, why not, why not,
Why not, why not, why not.

(*Shouted to orchestra*)   Shut up!

(*Sings*)   Bring nasty children back? Olé.

OLLY   Well there we are then. Now we know. Let's blow him off the stage. Bye-bye Herod.

(*Blows* HEROD *off stage.*)

HEROD   Aggghhh! (*Crash off stage*) Who parked those camels in the foyer-room!

OLLY   Well Chicago. You'd better be off too. Back to work.

CHICAGO   (*hesitant*) Olly.

OLLY   Yes Chicago?

CHICAGO   Can I have a change of job. I'm fed up with Herod. And I'm getting very bad. I smoke cigars. (*Takes cigar out of bowler.*)

OLLY   I know.

CHICAGO   And I'm the one who...

OLLY   ... makes all the burn holes in the clouds. (*Comes back downstage.*) But the point is Chicago—who's going to protect our friends from Herod if you don't?

CHICAGO   Anyone!

OLLY   But you're best at it.

CHICAGO	I'm not. I'm terrible at it.
OLLY	Ah. That's what you think—but listen.

(OLLY *to audience.*)

Are you glad Angel Chicago's protecting you from Herod?

(*Wait for reaction.*)

Is he good at it? (*To* CHICAGO) What more can I say?

CHICAGO	I'm good at it.

(OLLY *heads upstage.* ANGEL CHICAGO *follows.*)

I'm best at it.

OLLY	Go and find Herod!

(CHICAGO *watches* OLLY *until he's out of sight, then throws tantrum.*)

CHICAGO	I'm fed up! I'm fed up, fed up, fed up. (*Throws his bowler hat on the floor and jumps up and down on it*) I'm fed up, fed up, fed up.

(LOFTY, JELLY *and* ANGY *enter gather round* ANGEL CHICAGO. *Watching his tantrum with interest. The tantrum works itself out.* ANGEL CHICAGO *ends sitting cross-legged with beaten bowler on his head.*)

LOFTY	You're not very happy are you?
JELLY	Has someone said something to upset you?
CHICAGO	(*happy*) No. I'm fine now thanks. Just thought I'd get rid of a bit of tension. Let off a bit of steam. Clear my system a bit.
ANGY	What's tension, Chicago?
CHICAGO	You know Angy, when you get all bad-tempered. All tight inside. That's tension. You know?

(ANGY *shakes her head for* "*No I don't know*".)

Well *you* know Lofty don't you.

(LOFTY *shakes his head.*)

CHICAGO (Cont'd.)	Jelly?
	(JELLY *shakes her head.*)
	Oh. Well I know. Perhaps it's because of watching Herod. I thought we all got tense up here. I didn't realize I was the only one in Heaven who gets tense. (*Indicates the Audience*) I mean they get tense all the time. Don't you? They hear Herod coming and that's it. Rigid: shiver shiver. "Ugh, I hate nice boys and girls," he says. And that's it. Tense, tense, straight away. Don't you?
LOFTY	What's it like Chicago?
JELLY	Yeh. What's it like?
CHICAGO	Well—it's hard to explain. I'll tell you what—I'll show you.
	Music No. 7. "*TENSION*" (CHICAGO, HEROD, OLLY and CHORUS).
CHICAGO (*Spoken*)	When your arm goes like that— And your leg goes like that— And your back goes like that— That's tension, that's tension, That's, that's tension!
(*Sings*)	When your shoulders go like that— And your neck goes like that— That's tension, tension, tension. When your elbows go like that— And your knees go like that— That's tension, tension, tension.
	You feel it taking a grip— Your hold starts to slip— Tension, tension, tension— You feel it grabbing your bones, All of you moans That's tension, tension, tension.
	When your fingers go like that— And your toes go like that— That's tension, tension, tension!
	(*4 bars orchestra*)

CHICAGO ANGY, JELLY and LOFTY (*Unison*)	When your shoulders go like that— And your neck goes like that— That's tension, tension, tension. When your elbows go like that— And your knees go like that— Tension, tension, tension.
	You feel it taking a grip— Your hold starts to slip— Tension, tension, tension— You feel it grabbing your bones, All of you moans That's tension, tension, tension.
CHICAGO and CHORUS (*unis.*)	When your fingers go like this— And your toes go like this— That's tension, tension, tension.
	(*4 bars of music as 'plane sound effect is established.* MARY, JOSEPH *and* VILLAGERS *run on stage with their hands over their ears.*)
CHICAGO	When planes go like this— And trains go like this— That's tension, tension, tension! When police cars go like this— And Fire Engines go like this— That's tension, tension, tension!
ALL (*unis.*)	You feel it taking a grip— Your hold starts to slip— Tension, tension, tension! You feel it grabbing your bones, All of you moans, That's tension, tension, tension!
	When dogs go like this,
ANGELS	Woof Woof,
ALL	And cats go like this;
ANGELS	Mi-aow
ALL	That's tension, tension, tension!
	(*16 bars of music. Then* HEROD *and* TWO SOLDIERS *enter.*)

HEROD (*Sings*)   When your mouth goes like that—
And your eyes go like that—

ALL (*unis.*)   That's tension, tension, tension!

HEROD   When your teeth go like that—
And your throat goes like this (*Grrr!*)

ALL (*unis.*)   That's tension, tension, tension!

ALL (*harmony*)   You feel it taking a grip—
Your hold starts to slip—
Tension, tension, tension!
You feel it grabbing your bones,
All of you moans.
That's tension, tension, tension!

OLLY   When thunder goes like this—(*noise of thunder*)
And lightning goes like this—(*lightning*)

ALL   That's tension, tension, tension!

OLLY   When rain goes like this—

CHORUS   Pitter patter

OLLY   And the wind goes like this—

CHORUS   Whoo——sh

ALL   That's tension, tension, tension!

(*4 beats on drums*)

ALL (*spoken*)   When the Band plays like this!

(*8 bars of music from* **BAND**)

ALL (*Sung in harmony*)   That's tension, tension, tension!

ALL (*harmony*)   When hooters go like this—
And clocks go like this—
Tension, tension, tension!
When sirens go like this—
And drills go like this—
Tension, tension, tension!

(*4 bars rhythm from Orchestra*)

CHICAGO (*Shouts to Orchestra*) Shut up!

CHICAGO (*Spoken*) Arms, legs, hands, feet,
Head, shoulders, back and seat.
Mouth and kneecaps, tongue and hips,
Toes and teeth and shins and lips.
Eyelids, earholes, double chin,
Nose to let the smells pour in.
Heart and lungs and chest and tum,
Calves and thighs and great big bum.

ALL (*harmony*) Tension, tension, tension, tension!
Tension, tension, tension, tension!
Tension, tension, tension, tension!
Tension, Tension, Tension, Tension!
Tension!

(*Everybody collapses on the floor, apart from* OLLY.)

OLLY Right all of you, back to work. If you go on at this rate,
Mary won't have her baby by next Christmas.

(*Everybody leaves stage except* ANGEL CHICAGO, ANGY, JELLY *and* LOFTY.)

CHICAGO Now do you see what I mean?

ALL Yes.

ANGY I like it. Tension!

(ANGY *does a little tension dance*.)

CHICAGO Angy. Angy! We finished that one. Anyway, where are you off to?

LOFTY We're off to make three wise men decide that they should follow a star to Bethlehem, where Mary's going to have her baby.

JELLY I'm looking forward to it. We're not going to appear, we're just going to turn over pages and things in old books where the message is hidden.

ANGY Until they get the message. And then—tension!

(ANGY *does a little tension dance*.)

CHICAGO Angry! Attention!! Lucky old you lot. Oh well. I suppose I better go and find rotten old Herod. Let you get on with your job.
(HEROD *heard shouting off stage*.)

CHICAGO (Cont'd.)	Hello! It looks as though he's found me.
	(HEROD *enters stage left.*)
HEROD	Any volunteers for kick a camel for charity week? No—Well—
	Music No. 8. "*NICE BOYS AND GIRLS*" Reprise (HEROD).
HEROD (*Spoken*)	You're all Scurvy and slimy and sloppy and stupid, Hideously odious, obnoxious as cupid. You're putrid and pongy, and sickly as slugs, As plaguish as ants and as pleasant as bugs. Bugs! you naughty little fellow. You're all grisly and ghastly and glaringly gruesome, Putrescent, repellent, repulsively pukesome. Musty and monstrous and mouldy as mice, You're boringly—yawningly—horribly nice.
	(*Orchestra continues until lights up on* WISE MEN)
	(ANGEL CHICAGO *exits after* HEROD. JELLY, ANGY *and* LOFTY *exit opposite side.* BLACKOUT.)
	(*By now, upstage, the* THREE WISE MEN *sit at desks piled high with books, fast asleep. Snoring gently.* ANGY, LOFTY *and* JELLY *enter and go one behind each* KING.)
JELLY	Well are these the ones Lofty?
LOFTY	Yes. These are the three Wise men.
ANGY	They don't look very wise to me.
LOFTY	Well they are. Ever so bright! No-one looks very clever when they're asleep, now do they. Hey, don't Wise Men snore a lot?
JELLY	Shall we wake them up to stop the noise?
	(*Business.*)
LOFTY	No. Let's get the books on the right pages first. I've found my page.
ANGY	Hey, Lofty, my Wise Man's lying on his book and I can't move him. What shall I do?
LOFTY	Just tickle his nose with that feather, that'll get him moving.

ANGY	What a good idea. Tickle tickle tickle.

(*Business between* ANGY, WISE MAN *and quill pen.*)

JELLY	Hey! I've found my page.
ANGY	No. No. No. Yes! I've found mine!

(ANGY, JELLY *and* LOFTY *blow into the* WISE MEN's *ears. The* WISE MEN *stretch and wake. The* ANGELS *move down stage.*)

LOFTY	(*to audience*) Don't worry, they can't see us. Only you can. Now let's see how wise they really are.
1ST W. MAN	(*stands*) Eureka!
JELLY	What does Eureka mean Angy?
ANGY	I don't know—but they always say that.
1ST W. MAN	It is written, that a saviour is to be born.
2ND W. MAN	(*stands*) Eureka! Here it says he will be born in a stable.

(3RD WISE MAN *stands.*)

JELLY	Here we go again.
3RD W. MAN	Eureka! It says here a star will appear to show us the way.
ANGY **JELLY** **LOFTY**	Eureka!!
LOFTY	That's it. We've done our job. Let's be off.
1ST W. MAN	Look. The star!
2ND W. MAN **3RD W. MAN**	Where?
1ST W. MAN	Over there in the East.
2ND W. MAN	Hang on while I put my glasses on.
3RD W. MAN	I see it. I see it.
2ND W. MAN	Where? Over there?
1ST W. MAN	No it's moved... It's over there.

2ND W. MAN	Oh.
LOFTY	Do you reckon Gabby's messing about?
ANGY	No. I should imagine he's just getting the feel of it. It's not easy being a star.
3RD W. MAN	Let us be on our way.

(*The* WISE MEN *gather some possessions together to take with them.*)

JELLY	Hey! Don't you think it would be nice if they each took a present with them for the baby.
ANGY	What sort of thing?
JELLY	I don't know—just a present of some sort.
LOFTY	Perhaps this lot have some ideas. (*Speaks to the Audience*) Here! We think it might be nice if the Wise Men took a present each for the baby. Do you agree? What? Right. What do you think my Wise Man should take? That one there. Gold? Right. Hang on—I'll go and whisper.

Music No. 8a. "*MAGIC SOUNDS*"

(LOFTY *goes and whispers in the* WISE MAN'*s ear.*)

1ST W. MAN	I think I shall take a present for the baby. I shall take gold.
ANGY	Very good Lofty. (*To Audience*) Now what about mine, what shall he take? What? Frank who? Frank*incense*—right. Hang on.

Repeat Music No. 8a.

(ANGY *goes and whispers in* 2ND WISE MAN'*s ear.*)

2ND W. MAN	I think that I also shall take a present for the baby. I shall take Frankincense.
LOFTY	Well done Angy. Go on Jelly, see what they think yours should take.
JELLY	Right. Now we've had gold, and we've had Frankincense—what do you think my Wise Man should take? Myrrh!? What's that? Never heard of it. Myrrh? What is it? Do you know what it is Lofty?

LOFTY	Never heard of it.
JELLY	What about you Angy?
ANGY	I think it's a sort of horse.
JELLY	Is it a sort of horse? No. Well is it a Lord Mayor or something? No. Well I'll just tell him. I'll just tell my Wise Man and see what he makes of it—hang on.

Repeat Music No. 8a.

(JELLY *goes and whispers in* 3RD WISE MAN's *ear.*)

3RD W. MAN	I also shall take a present for the baby. I shall take Myrrh.
1ST W. MAN **2ND W. MAN**	What's that?
3RD W. MAN	It's a transparent yellow-brown gum resin used as incense.
1ST W. MAN **2ND W. MAN** **LOFTY** **ANGY** **JELLY**	Pardon?
3RD W. MAN	It's for making a nice smell.
1ST W. MAN **2ND W. MAN**	Oh!
JELLY	Hey—you were right Lofty. They are wise aren't they.

Repeat Music No. 8a. (*last time*)

LOFTY	Yeh. I told you. Come on let's go and tell Olly we've done the job all right.
ANGELS	(*whispers to Wise Men*) Follow the star.

(ANGY, JELLY *and* LOFTY *return to heaven, after having struck tables and books.* THREE KINGS *set off on their journey.*)

Music No. 9. "*FOLLOW THE STAR*" (THREE WISE MEN *with* GABBY *and* OFF-STAGE CHORUS).

ALL KINGS	We are going to find a King	
GABBY	Follow the star, follow the star	
ALL KINGS	We shall take three precious things.	
GABBY	Follow the star, follow the star	
		CHORUS (off-stage)
1ST KING	Gold for a crown	Ah
2ND KING	Frankincense fair	....
3RD KING	For the baby	Ah
	I shall take	Ah
	Myrrh.	Ah
2ND KING	Where shall we find this	....
	Saviour child?	Ah
3 KINGS and GABBY	Follow the star,	Follow the star,
	Follow the star.	Follow the star.
2ND KING	Gifts we shall take for the	Ah
	Baby so mild.	Ah
3 KINGS and GABBY	Follow the star,	Follow the star,
	Follow the star.	Follow the star.
1ST KING	Gold for a crown	Ah
2ND KING	Frankincense fair	....
3RD KING	For the baby	Ah
	I shall take	Ah
	Myrrh.	Ah
3RD KING	When we have finally	....
	Found him there	Ah
3 KINGS and GABBY	Follow the star,	Follow the star,
	Follow the star.	Follow the star.
3RD KING	Gifts we shall give this	Ah
	Saviour fair.	Ah
3 KINGS and GABBY	Follow the star,	Follow the star,
	Follow the star.	Follow the star.
1ST KING	Gold for a Crown,	Ah
2ND KING	Frankincense fair,	....
3RD KING	For the baby	Ah
	I shall take	Ah
	Myrrh.	Ah
3RD KING		**GABBY, 1ST and 2ND KING and CHORUS**
	Follow the star,	Follow the star,

3RD KING (Cont'd.)	GABBY, 1ST and 2ND KING and CHORUS (Cont'd.)
Follow the star,	Follow the star,

(*Keep repeating till* KINGS *exit.*)

(MARY *and* JOSEPH *on stage.* MARY *obviously pregnant.*)

(*Upstage,* VILLAGERS *from Nazareth enter grumbling.*)

(MARY *goes to lift something heavy.*)

JOSEPH   Careful now.

MARY   I'll be alright.

(ZACHARIUS *enters bad tempered.*)

JOSEPH   What's the matter today, Zacharius?

ZAC   Well, I think it's all wrong. Hello, Joseph.

JOSEPH   Hi.

ZAC   Why should we go all the way to Bethlehem just to sign our name in a rotten book, and say we belong to the family of David? I think it's all wrong. Why should we?

2ND VILLAGER   Because he's ordered it Zacharias, that's why.

ZAC   Well it's not good enough, that's what I say.

3RD VILLAGER   It'd better be, otherwise you'll just end up in prison.

2ND VILLAGER   I don't understand. Why we should all go. Why can't just one of us go and sign for everybody in the village.

JOSEPH   Because that's not the way you do it. We've all got to go to Bethlehem.

ZAC   Well I think it's all wrong. That's what I think.

(*Girl enters.*)

GIRL   Hello Joseph. Hello Mary.

MARY/JOSEPH   Hello.

ZAC	Well, I'm not going!
JOSEPH	Our King, David, has demanded it. That's good enough for me, and it should be for you.
ZAC	Well what about poor Mary here, the journey's not going to be much fun for her, is it.
MARY	Oh. I'm alright Zac. Anyway, I don't suppose we're being made to go there for fun. King David wants to know how many people he's got in the Kingdom, that's all.
2ND VILLAGER	I think just a couple of villagers should go to sign for everybody. That's what I think.

(*Disagreement etc. to cover moves.*)

JOSEPH	Stop beefing. We've got to go—let's go with a smile.
MARY	Come on, before you know it, we'll have been and be back. Keep cheery about it.
GIRL	You just wait Mary. I bet if you start having your baby when we're on the way, or when we get there, you won't be so cheery.
JOSEPH	Mary'll be all right. Don't you worry.
MARY	Of course I will.
ZAC	Mm! You just wait, time will tell.
MARY	Joseph, do you think I might have the baby on the way?
JOSEPH	No. You'll be fine, Mary. We'll be back in no time.
MARY	I hope so, Joseph. I want to have my baby at home.
JOSEPH	You will, Mary. You will.

Music No. 10. "*HOME*" (**MARY**, **JOSEPH** *and* **CHORUS**).

MARY	Home—where we can stretch and scratch and feel so at ease
JOSEPH	Home—where no-one stares and points when you sit down and show your knees!
MARY	Home—where we know ev'ryone and greet them in the street (*spoken*) Hello, Vera!

JOSEPH	Home—where we take off our shoes and walk around in bare feet!	
MARY and JOSEPH		**CHORUS**
		Ah
	I know it's	....
	Not very posh and the	Ah
	Carpets are a little bare,	Ah
	.... But when	Ah
	We feel really low,	Ah
	.... Don't we	Ah
	Wish that we	Ah
	Were there (by the fire-side).	

MARY and JOSEPH   Home—where we can sing and shout and do just what we please,
Home—that is the only place where we really feel at home!

DANCE (*Players on stage play percussion instruments.*)

JOSEPH (*Spoken*)   And now, at enormous expense!

(*Music continues*)

MARY and JOSEPH		**CHORUS**
		Ah
	I know, seeing new places	....
	Can be a lot of	Ah
	Fun, but, when we feel	Ah
	Really down, where's the place that	Ah
	We want to run to?	
	Home,	Home,
	Where we know ev'ryone,	Where we know ev'ryone,
	And greet them in the street	And greet them in the street
JOSEPH (*Spoken*)	Hello, Lynne!	....
MARY and JOSEPH	Home,	Home,
	That is the only place	That is the only place
	Where we really feel at,	Where we really feel at,
	Where we really feel at,	
	Where we really feel at home!	Where we really feel at home!

JOSEPH (*Spoken*)   Let's go! First stop—Bethlehem.

(*Orchestra continues during exit*)

(VILLAGERS *and* MARY *and* JOSEPH *exit. Enter the* THREE WISE MEN *led by* GABBY.)

1ST W. MAN   Let's rest a-while. My feet are killing me. (*Sits*)

2ND W. MAN   (*Sniffing*) They're killing me as well. (*Sits*)

3RD W. MAN	We have travelled many days. What lands have we now reached?
2ND W. MAN	The lands of Herod.
3RD W. MAN	Oh he's very nice. Very nice indeed.
	(*Play it by ear until* HEROD *is heard off-stage with* ANGEL CHICAGO *not far behind.*)
HEROD	RANT! ROAR! All these creepies still here, etc . . . (*Ad lib*)
3RD W. MAN	Ah. I think I hear him approaching now.
	(HEROD *enters and stops ranting when he sees the* WISE MEN. ANGEL CHICAGO *follows.*)
HEROD	(*aside*) Who's this that dares cross my land?
CHICAGO	Hello! What have we here.
HEROD	Who are you?
1ST W. MAN	We
2ND W. MAN	three kings
3RD W. MAN	from Orient
ALL W. MEN	Ah!
HEROD	Ah! Foreigners.
1ST W. MAN	We have come far Herod. We are following a star to a place where a baby will be born.
HEROD	A baby?
3RD W. MAN	He will be our saviour.
HEROD	Our saviour?
2ND W. MAN	A new King.
HEROD	A new King? (*Clenched teeth smile*) *How* simply lovely. (*Turns and glowers at Audience. Then goes into a huddle with the* WISE MEN.)

CHICAGO Oh dear! Now there'll be trouble.

(HEROD *reacts to the* KINGS' *news.* ANGEL CHICAGO *walks downstage and sings to the Audience.*)

Music No. 11. *"WE WON'T LET THE BABY DIE"* (CHICAGO, HEROD, THREE KINGS *and* CHORUS).

CHICAGO (*Sings*) Herod doesn't like the things
That he's being told by the three Kings,
I can see in his eyes that the news is driving him wild!

HEROD (*Shouted*) Wild! Wild! Wild!

CHICAGO He is such a wicked man,
Already he's forming some evil plan,
Thinking of how he can harm the unborn child.

(HEROD *moves downstage to Audience.*)

HEROD (*Sings*) I'll make that baby sigh. I'll make that baby cry.
I'll make that baby sigh. I'll make that baby die!

(*To* WISE MEN)
I'm very pleased to hear your news,
Now a lovely little present I will go and choose
To take along with me when I visit this new-born King.
You three go ahead and follow the star,
And perhaps when you find him, if it's not too far,
You can come back here and tell me where he is.

(*To Audience*)
I'll make that baby sigh. I'll make that baby cry.
I'll make that baby sigh. I'll make that baby die!

(*Draws his sword.*)
It's nice to know there's a new King around,
Now a suitable present I think I've found,
And I'm sure my present will be a big surprise!
Shining bright and beautiful is this thing
That I'll go along and give to the King.

I can't wait to see the look in the little child's eyes!

CHICAGO	**THREE KINGS**
We won't	
Let the baby die, we won't	Ah
Let the baby die,	Ah
	Ah

CHICAGO (Cont'd.)	THREE KINGS (Cont'd.)
We won't let the baby die,	....
	Ah
We won't let the baby die.	....

(*Calls to the other* ANGELS:—)

(*Shouted*) GABBY! OLLY! JELLY! LOFTY! ANGY! All of you. Trouble!

(ANGELS *start arriving.*)

(HEROD *sings to Audience.*)

HEROD	KINGS and CHORUS
I'll	
Follow those men and I'll find the	Ah
King, and then I'll do a very evil	....
Thing,	....
Something that will really make me	Ah
Smile!	....
I'll	
Go along and be very bad,	Ah
I will kill that little lad. That'll	....
Teach him not to try to cramp my	Ah
Style.	....
I'll	
Make that baby sigh.	Ah
	Ah
I'll make that baby cry.	....
	Ah
I'll make that baby sigh.	....
	Ah
I'll make that baby die!	....
	We won't let the baby die!
I'll make that baby	....
Sigh!	We won't let the baby die!
I'll make that baby	....
Die!	We won't let the baby die!

(*Repeat until* OLLY *blows whistle and shouts.*)

OLLY (**Shouts**) STOP!

(*Everyone on stage freezes.*)

OLLY Now you're going to frighten everyone if you're not careful. So stop it. (*Turns to Audience*) I tell you what. You all go off now and have an ice-cream or orange or something, and by the time you get back I'll try to have something worked out. All right? Right. Off you go then. I'll see you in about fifteen minutes. (*Calling*) Right!

(*1 bar Orchestra into*)

ALL (*except*   We won't let the baby die,
HEROD) (*sing*)   We won't let the baby die!

(*and repeat ad lib. as all* EXIT.)

CURTAIN FALLS

END OF ACT ONE

AD LIB.
(*During Interval* HEROD *meanders through bars and foyer, trying to get children on his side, to drink strong drink,*
(ANGEL CHICAGO *follows, telling him to be good, protecting the kids, etc.*)

ACT II

Music No. 12. "*ENTR'ACTE*" (Orchestra).

(ANGEL CHICAGO *enters towards end of interval. Chats to Audience, then goes to top level.*)

CHICAGO   I've never been up here before! Here, have you seen Olly? Is Olly back yet? Oh, I'll have a sly smoke while I'm waiting.

(*Business with Cigar and Light.*)

You lot mustn't smoke. If you do you'll grow up to be dwarfs. Bit naughty, isn't it. Smoking. Bit naughty. Anyway you've go to be a little bit naughty sometimes, haven't you. And did you know, how naughty you are depends what sort you are. "Careful, Carefree or Careless". Here, I'll show you what I mean.

Music No. 13. "*CAREFUL, CAREFREE OR CARELESS*" (CHICAGO).

CHICAGO (*Sings*)   If you were walking around,
                           And you saw a hole in the ground,
                           Would you walk right round,
                           Jump over, or jump in? Ah—Ha!

                           It depends what type you are,
                           It depends what type you are,
                           Careful, carefree or careless,
                           It depends what type you are.

CHICAGO (*Sings*)
(**Cont'd.**)
If your mother bought a new hat,
And said, "What do you think of that?"
Would you say, "It's nice",
Tell the truth, or just say "Yak!"

If your dad bought a bright yellow suit,
And said "Do you think this is cute?"
Would you say, "It's nice",
Tell the truth or just say—(*Dirty laugh*)

It depends what type you are,
It depends what type you are,
Careful, carefree or careless,
It depends what type you are.

(*8 bars "Scat" singing then*)

(DANCE)

CHICAGO (*Sings*) If you saw a bull eating grass,
In a field that you had to pass,
Would you go another way, walk round
Or kick him up the behind?

So if *you* are walking around,
And *you* see a hole in the ground,
Will you walk right round,
Jump over, or jump in? Oh, Yeah!

It depends what type you are,
It depends what type you are,
Careful, carefree or careless,
It depends what type you are.

La, la, la, la, la, la,
It depends, what type, you are,
Da, da, da, da, da, da, da, da.
Yeah!

(OLLY *enters at houselights to half. Speaks to Audience.*)

OLLY Right. Are you all back then? Have a look beside you, see if everyone's there who should be. If you're with a grown up—be sure you've got the right one. Just have a check. I don't want you all to spend half the second act trying to swap the grown up you've found for the one you've put down somewhere. Have a check?— Good. Alright? Now—have you all been? Good. (*Etc. until Audience is settled*) Right. Now the second act sets off quietly. Mary

OLLY (Cont'd.) and Joseph have arrived in Bethlehem, and they're looking for somewhere to stay,—so keep your voices down at the beginning; we don't want to frighten the Inn Keepers, do we? Anyway, you'll get a chance to shout later. Right. Are you all settled?

O.K. Houselights out!

Music No. 14. *"THERE IS NO ROOM"* (ANGY, JELLY, LOFTY *and* CHORUS, OFF-STAGE).

(MARY *and* JOSEPH *enter right and meander from door to door, acting out the song.*)

ANGY
Have you ever felt lonely?
Have you ever felt tired?
Have you ever felt lost
With no place to go?
Well, think of Joseph,
Lost in a strange town,
Searching for a bed
Where the baby could be born.

ANGY	**LOFTY and JELLY**
You can't come in!	Ah
You can't come in!	Ah
You can't stay here, there's no	Ah
Room in this	Ah
Inn!	Ah

And think of Mary,
Her time was near now,
Saying to Joseph,
"What can we do?"
"Don't worry, Mary,
We'll find a room soon,
We'll soon find
A room in an Inn".

ALL THREE
You can't come in,
You can't come in,
You can't stay here,
There's no room in this Inn!

(*Key change*)

ANGY	"Please, can you help us? The town is crowded. We just need a bed for the night. My wife is pregnant. She's very near now. We must find a bed for the night".
ALL THREE	You can't come in, You can't come in, You can't stay here, There's no room in this Inn!

ANGY		**LOFTY and JELLY**
	From door to door, ... From street to street, ... Always the Answer,	From door to door, ... From street to street, ... Always
	"No room in this Inn". Then one took Pity Said "There's a Stable, It isn't Much But it's all that I have".	"No room in this Inn". . . . . Then one took Pity, Said "There's a Stable It is all that I have".

ALL THREE	You can't come in, You can't come in, Use the stable, There's no room in this Inn.

(Key change)

ANGY	Early that morning, As daylight was dawning, There in the stable A baby was born. His name was Jesus, He came to save us. Open your hearts. And let him come in!
ALL THREE	There must be room! There must be room! Open your hearts, And let him come in!

ANGY		LOFTY and JELLY
		Ah
	Have you ever felt lonely?	. . . . . .
		Ah
	Have you ever felt tired?	. . . . . .
		Ah
	Have you ever felt lost, with	. . . . . .
	No-where to go?	Ah
	Well, think of Je-	
	. . . .	Well,
	Sus,	Think of Je-
	He came to	Sus,
	Save us,	He came to
	Open your	Save us,
	Hearts, and	Open your
	Let him come in!	Hearts to him!

ALL THREE and   There must be room!
CHORUS   There must be room!
                         Open your hearts,
                         And let him come in!

(BLACKOUT)

(*Orchestra continues till lights up*)

(*A baby cries.*)

(*At the end of song* MARY *and* JOSEPH *are left sitting either side of crib.* OXY *and* ASS *stand chewing, stage left. Downstage of them,* ANGY, LOFTY *and* JELLY *hold conference.*)

ANGY   They look very fed up don't they?

LOFTY   Oxes and asses always look fed up—I think it's all that chewing they do. (*Imitates them*)

OXY   Watch it Lofty.

ASS   Yeh. Watch it or we'll tell Olly next time we see him. Taking the micky out of us.

ANGY   No, I'm not talking about Oxy and Assy, I'm talking about Mary and Joseph. Don't they look fed up?

JELLY   Well, you'd look fed up too if you'd travelled as far as they have. And when you got there you found there was nowhere to stay. And you ended up having your baby in a stable, now wouldn't you?

ANGY	Yes, I suppose so.
OXY	My mother had her baby in a stable, and she wasn't fed up.
ASS	So did mine. Mine was quite pleased in fact. She hated proper beds. Said they brought her out in a rash.
JELLY	Well you're both different aren't you. I mean you're animals. They're humans. They're not used to stables like you are.
LOFTY	Yeh. I suppose it must be a bit funny. Anyway, what are we going to do about it.
ANGY	I don't know what we can do. I tell you what, shall we appear to them and have a chat?
JELLY	No we can't. Olly would be furious.
OXY	I'd tell them some of my jokes,—but they don't seem to like ox tales.
ASS	I'd sing them a song—but humans don't seem to like my songs. (*Gives a bray*)
LOFTY	I've got it! It's simple. We'll ask this lot.
JELLY / **ANGY**	Of course. (*Move downstage.*)
LOFTY	Now here's the problem. Mary and Joseph are a bit fed up because they've got no one to talk to, and they're all by themselves in a strange stable. Now can you suggest anyone who might come and talk to them. Or better still a few people. You know, people looking after cows nearby or donkeys something like that.

(*Play it by ear until the* **SHEPHERDS** *are established.*)

JELLY	Shepherds? Well, where are they? You what? On a hill. Oh.
ANGY	What are they doing there? (*either*) Washing their socks? (*or*)— Looking after their feet? Oh! Watching their flocks! Oh! Looking after their sheep! Come on then Jelly, come on Lofty, let's go and get them.
LOFTY	Yeah. Oxy and Assy. You keep an eye on things here until we get back. O.K?
OXY and ASS	O.K.

JELLY (*To Audience*)	Will you all shout out if the baby's in danger at all? All right?
ANGY	Yes, if you see Herod coming, let Oxy and Assy know. O.K.? Let's go. 'Bye, everyone, see you soon.
OXY and ASS	'Bye, Angy, Jelly, Lofty.
OXY	(*pause*) Well, Assy? (*Pause*) What shall we do while we're waiting?
ASSY	(*pause*) How about doing our little dance.
OXY	A good idea, Assy.

(*They dance to "Careful, Carefree, Careless".*)

Music No. 15. "*DANCE*" (OXY and ASSY).

(KING HEROD *appears at downstage right. Doesn't see* MARY, JOSEPH *and* BABY, *and* OX *and* ASS *don't see him.*) (*Music fades*)

HEROD	(*evil whisper*) I'm going to find the baby and kill him. (*Ad lib.*)

(*Play it by ear until the audience draws their attention—by which time* HEROD *has gone.*)

ASSY	They're kidding us.

Music No. 15 Continued (*Letter C*) (*7 bars only*) (*Music stops.*)

OXY	Are you taking the mickey out of me?
ASSY	Och, no!

(*Music continues* (*Letter D*) (*17 bars*)

(ANGEL CHICAGO *enters.*)

CHICAGO	Hello, Oxy. Hello, Assy. I'm fed up.
OXY	Why, Chicago?
CHICAGO	It's rotten old King Herod. He's fooling me now by not shouting, and I'm having an awful job finding him.
OXY	Well, they said he was here a minute ago, but we looked everywhere and couldn't find him.
ASS	They said he was down here, but when we looked he wasn't there.

CHICAGO Where did you say he was? etc. (*Ad lib. play by ear*)

(*As they move downstage right* HEROD *creeps in stage left.*)

HEROD (*whispering*) I'm going to find him. I hate boys and girls, but most of all I hate babies! Boo! Yourself! Nasty Creepies! I'll try down here!

(*Play it by ear until audience draws* CHICAGO's *attention.*)

CHICAGO I'm sure you're right, but he's not there now. Aw, is that . . . is that the baby Jesus in the crib? I'll go and say hello.

(ANGEL CHICAGO *moves upstage to crib.* CHICAGO "Itchy-coo's" *the Baby.*)

(*loudly*) Hello! Itchy coo! Itchy coo!

(*Offstage* HEROD *gives a giant shout.*)

HEROD (*offstage*) I'll find him! I'll find the baby.

CHICAGO It is Herod! Quick. Oxy and Assy, hide Mary and Joseph and the baby.

(OX, ASS *and* ANGEL CHICAGO *spread themselves so as to hide* MARY, JOSEPH *and crib.* HEROD *comes on stage.*)

HEROD (*oozing niceness*) Hello boys and girls. I wonder if you'd like to help me. Yes of course you would. Now—will you tell me where the baby is? There you'd like to do that wouldn't you. Oh yes you would.
(*Getting more bad tempered*) Oh yes you would. Tell me you rotten smelly lot. Tell me! I don't need your help. I'll find him myself.

(*as if calling a kitten*)
Here baby, baby, baby.
Here baby, baby—
Got a little present for you.
Itchy-coo, itchy-coo, itchy-coo.
Here little baby. Where are you hiding?

(HEROD *reaches crib but it's now empty as* CHICAGO *has removed baby.*)

Ah! . . . Gone!
Where are you? Nice King Herod's looking for you. Here baby.
(*shouts*) Where are you, you grotty little imposter.
(*to* OXY) Go away, or I'll make you into cubes.

HEROD (Cont'd.) I'll find you finally!
I'll finally find you.
And when I find you finally—I'll shred you!

(HEROD *exits.*)

CHICAGO That was a close thing. Congratulations, Oxy and Assy. Well done. (*Gives a little bow*)

OXY And well done you, Chicago.

ASSY Now we've got a bit of peace, perhaps we can finish our dance.

OXY Good idea, Assy.

CHICAGO A dance? Oh, I love dancing, can you teach me before I go?

ASS Of course, Chicago. A pleasure. After you, Oxy.

CHICAGO Oh, thank you, I've always wanted to do an oxtrot.

Music No. 15 Continued (*Letter E to end of number*).

(OX, ASS *and* CHICAGO *do a simple dance.*) (*Tango, follow by Polka*)

(*Lights fade.*)

(BLACKOUT.)

Music No. 15a—To open Shepherd Scene.

(*Lights up on* SHEPHERDS *watching their flocks.* SHEPHERDS *are ad-libbing among themselves. Doing little chores, sitting around, relaxed. Perhaps one plays a flute.* (Flute in orchestra) *Socks are hanging on clothes line.*)

(LOFTY *appears, high, stage left.*)

LOFTY Shepherds!—Shush!

(SHEPHERDS *don't hear him.*)

Shepherds!—Shush!

3RD SHEPHERD It's an angel!

(*Silence falls*)

LOFTY   I've got some good news for you lot—you are cordially invited to come and have a chat with a new born baby King and his mum and dad, in a stable in Bethlehem.

1ST SHEPHERD   Eh! That's not an angel. It's just Charlie Stephen's boy dressed up to fool us.

2ND SHEPHERD   Well done, boy. You really had us fooled for a minute. I was even starting to believe perhaps a new King had been born!

LOFTY   I am an angel! A new King has been born! Look at that star up there, zig-zagging down and up, down and up, down and up, that shines where the King's been born. I am an angel!

3RD SHEPHERD   Well, I'll believe it when I see some more like you.

LOFTY   Angels! Arrive!

Music No. 16. *"A BABY'S BEEN BORN"* (*"Angels' Song"*) (ANGY, JELLY, LOFTY *and* THREE SHEPHERDS).

ANGY	**JELLY**	**LOFTY**
A baby's		
Been born!	A baby's	
A baby's been born!	Been born, been born!	A baby's been born!
		Come and see,
Come and see,		Come and see,
Come and see	Come and see	Come and see
Where the baby's	Where the baby's	Where the baby's
Been born!	Been born!	Been born!
ANGY and 3RD SHEPHERD (*Tenor*)	**JELLY and 2ND SHEPHERD** (*Tenor*)	**LOFTY and 1ST SHEPHERD** (*Bass*)
		A new King's
	A new King's	Been born,
A new King's been born!	Been born, been born!	A new King's been born!
		Come and see,
	Come and see,	Come and see,
Come and see	Come and see	Come and see
Where the new King's	Where the new King's	Where the new King's
Been born!	Been born!	Been born!

(*Blackout at end of song—Exit* SHEPHERDS *and* ANGELS.)

(*Still in Blackout,* MARY *cries out.*)

(*Orchestra continues under dialogue*)

MARY (*frightened*) Joseph! (*Pause*) Joseph! Quickly!

(*Lights up.* MARY *wide-eyed beside crib.* JOSEPH *rushes on stage.*)

JOSEPH (*worried*) What is it, Mary?

(MARY *still seeing her dream doesn't reply.*)

Mary! Tell me . . . What is it?

MARY (*long pause*) Our son, Joseph. Our son. They're going to kill him.

JOSEPH What are you talking about, Mary? We're here. We'll protect him. Nobody's going to hurt him. He's safe.

MARY Not now. It's not now, Joseph. When he grows up. I had a dream. So real—it was like being there. Oh, Joseph, when he grows up they're going to kill him. (*Music stops*)

JOSEPH It's just a dream, Mary.

MARY So real. His whole life.

Music No. 17. "*WE'LL ALWAYS LOVE HIM*" (MARY, JOSEPH *and* CHORUS OFF-STAGE).

MARY (*Sings*)
I dreamt our boy grew up to be a man
Like any other man we know,
And one day he came and said to us,
"Mum and Dad, it's time when I must go.

It is time when I must go and spread
The word among my flock, as my Father said, my Father said"
Joseph, very shortly after that
I dreamt I saw him dead. I saw him dead.

JOSEPH
We'll always love him,
We'll always care,
As long as he needs us,
We'll always be there.

MARY
I heard him preach the word
About a Kingdom where we all will finally be
And I heard him say that Heaven, where my Father lives,
Will open up for me.

MARY (Cont'd.)	Then I saw the priests and soldiers take him Roughly, to a man who wouldn't see, Who wouldn't see, Who took water in a bowl and said, "Jesus—I wash my hands of thee, my hands of thee."
JOSEPH	We'll always love him, We'll always care, As long as he needs us, We'll always be there.

(Key change)

MARY	Oh, Joseph, then I saw our child being followed by the people of that town Dragging up a hill so steep, a heavy cross of wood that really bore him down. And upon his head they had placed a crown of thorns, His back was lashed and bare, lashed and bare, And upon that hill they nailed him to a cross— And, Joseph, he died there. Our son died there.
JOSEPH and MALE CHORUS	We'll always love him, We'll always care, As long as he needs us, We'll always be

(Key change)

MARY		**FULL CHORUS**
	Joseph, I know it's just a dream,	Ah
	But while I slept it all seemed so real,	. . . .
		So real!
	And I	
	Know you think I'm foolish,	Ah
	But I thought I'd just tell you how I	. . . .
	Feel. That I	Ah
	Want our baby to be loved	Ah
	By ev'rybody here who hears me	. . . .
	Sing, who hears me sing. I want the	Ah
	World to go on loving him,	Ah
	Even if the soldiers do this	. . . .
	Thing, this evil thing!	Ah.
JOSEPH (*Spoken*)	We will, Mary. Don't worry—He'll be all right.	
MARY (*Spoken*)	Do you mean it, Joseph?	

JOSEPH (*Spoken*) He'll be all right.

JOSEPH and MARY (*Sing*)　　　　　　　　　　　**FULL CHORUS**

We'll always love him,	Ah
We'll always care, as	Ah
Long as he needs us, we'll	Ah
Always be	Ah
There. We'll be	Ah
There	Ah
As long as he needs us	As long as he needs us, we'll
We'll be	Be
There!	There! We'll be there!

(*At end of song they sit staring at the crib.*)

(*After a pause "ANGEL SONG" is heard being sung offstage by* **SHEPHERDS** *and* ANGELS *getting nearer.*)

Music No. 18. "*A BABY'S BEEN BORN*" (*Angels' Song*) (ANGY, JELLY, LOFTY, THREE SHEPHERDS *and* CHORUS).

ANGY (*Off-stage, no orchestra*)
A baby's been born!
A baby's been born!

　　　　　　　　　　　　　(*Dialogue under*)

Come and see,	**JOSEPH**	What is that, Mary?
Come and See,	**MARY**	I don't know. It sounds like singing. It's getting nearer.
Come and see		
Where the baby's	**OXY**	(*to* ASSY) Oh no! Not a party! I've got to go to work tomorrow.
Been born!		

(*Orchestra stars*)

(ANGY, JELLY, LOFTY *and* SHEPHERDS *pour into stable singing.*)

JELLY and SOPRANOS	ANGY and ALTOS	2ND and 3RD SHEPHERDS and TENORS	LOFTY and BASSES
			A new King's Been born,
A new King's been Born!	A new King's been Born!	A new King's Been born!	Been born!
		. . . .	. . . .
			Come and see,
Come and see	Come and see	Come and see,	Come and see,
Where the new	Where the new	Come and see	Come and see
King's been	King's been	Where the new	Where the new
Born.	Born.	King's been	King's been
Our Saviour's	Our Saviour's	Born, been born.	Born, been born.

JELLY and SOPRANOS Cont.	**ANGY and ALTOS Contd.**	**2ND and 3RD SHEPHERDS and TENORS Contd.**	**LOFTY and BASSES Contd.**
Been born!	Been born!	Our Saviour's	Our Saviour's
Our Saviour's	Our Saviour's	Been born!	Been born!
Been born!	Been born!	Our Saviour!	Our Saviour!
			Come and see,
		Come and see,	Come and see,
Come and see	Come and see	Come and see	Come and see
Where the baby's	Where the baby's	Where the baby's	Where the baby's
Been born!	Been born!	Been born, been born!	Been born, been born!
			A new King's
			Been born,
A new King's	A new King's	A new King,	A new King,
Been born,	Been born,	A Saviour!	A Saviour!
A Saviour!	A saviour!		A new King's
			Been born,
A new King,	A new King,	A new King,	A new-born
A new-born	A new-born	A new-born	Saviour!
Saviour!	Saviour!	Saviour!	A new King's
			Been born,
		A new King's	Been born!
		Been born!	. . . .
A new King's been	A new King's been	. . . .	Come and see,
Born!	Born!	Come and see,	Come and see,
		Come and see	Come and see
Come and see	Come and see	Where the new	Where the new
Where the new	Where the new	King's been	King's been
King's been	King's been	Born, been born.	Born, been born.
Born.	Born.		
Our Saviour's	Our Saviour's	Our Saviour's	Our Saviour's
Been born!	Been born!	Been born!	Been born!
Our Saviour's	Our Saviour's	Our Saviour!	Our Saviour!
Been born!	Been born!		Come and see,
		Come and see,	Come and see,
Come and see,	Come and see,	Come and see,	Come and see,
Come and see,	Come and see,	Come and see,	Come and see,
Our Saviour,	Our Saviour,	Our Saviour,	Our Saviour,
Our Saviour	Our Saviour	Our Saviour	Our Saviour
Is born!	Is born!	Is born!	Is born!

ANGY   Oh this is nice! Hello! Here comes Gabby to join us.

(*The* ANGELS *look up into the sky—their heads follow the motion of the unseen star as it descends erratically and finally lands with a crash off stage.*)
He did it very well for a beginner didn't he.
(GABBY *enters, noticeably taller. The* SHEPHERDS *go on chatting to* MARY *and* JOSEPH. OXY *and* ASSY *go on chewing.*)

GABBY	Hello everybody!
ALL THE ANGELS	Hello Gabby. You were a lovely star. You're ever so much taller. (*Etc*)
GABBY	It's ever so nice being a bit bigger. I must have been quite good. I only lost them once—in the mountains. But I went back and found them all right. They're just round the corner. They'll be here in a sec. I thought I'd pop ahead and see the baby. Who were all those people?
LOFTY	Mary and Joseph were a bit lonely, so everyone suggested we went and brought some shepherds back to talk to them.
GABBY	What a good idea. (*To Audience*) Aren't you clever.
JELLY	They're ever so nice, and the baby's lovely. Come and have a look.
GABBY	Right. Hello Oxy. Hello Assy.
OXY	Hello Gabby.
ASS	Hello Gabby. Thought you were never going to speak.
GABBY	Sorry Assy. I'm still excited at getting the three Wise Men here in one piece. Oxy, could you come over here and keep an eye open for them, they'll be here in a sec. I'm just going to look at the baby.

(GABBY *crosses to crib*.)

ANGY	Isn't this exciting.
LOFTY	Yes. It's lovely isn't it. Shall we give Olly a shout to come and join us?
JELLY	Yes. Why not. Get him away from head office for a bit.
ANGY **JELLY** **LOFTY**	(*musically*) Olly.

(OLLY *arrives spectacularly*.)

OLLY	Ah! So there you all are. I was wondering why heaven was so peaceful at the moment. It's paradise up here. What's going on?
LOFTY	Well, everything's just about organized Olly. The baby's been born. The shepherds come to visit. And we're expecting the three Wise Men to arrive any minute.

OLLY	Lovely! I see angel Gabriel's back. Looking tall and distinguished.
GABBY	Hello Olly. Thanks for giving me a second chance, and that lovely job. You come over here and see baby Jesus. He's smiling at me!

(OLLY *crosses to crib. In the distance the* WISE MEN *can be heard singing the chorus of* "Follow the Star".)

OXY   Hey. Gabby! The Kings are here!

(KINGS *enter still singing. Silence falls.*)

Music No. 19. "FOLLOW THE STAR" — Reprise (THREE WISE MEN).

THREE WISE MEN (*No orchestra*)

1ST KING	2ND and 3RD KINGS
We are going to	We are going to
Find a King.	Find a King.
Follow the star,	Ah
Follow the star.	Ah
We shall take three	We shall take three
Precious things.	Precious things.
Follow the star,	Ah
Follow the star.	Ah.

(*Orchestra under dialogue*)

OXY   Hey, Gabby! The Kings are here!
(KINGS *enter still singing.*)

Silence falls (*Orchestra continues*)

1ST WISE MAN   I have brought a gift for the new born King.
I have brought gold.

(*Everyone* "Ooohs!" *and* "Ahhs!")

(1ST WISE MAN *crosses to crib. Lays his gift down. Greets* MARY *and* JOSEPH *and* "Itchy coos" *to the* BABY.)

2ND WISE MAN   I also have brought a gift for the new born King.
I have brought Frankincense.

(*Everyone* "Ooohs!" *and* "Ahhhs!".)

(2ND WISE MAN *crosses to crib. Lays his gift down. Greets* MARY *and* JOSEPH *and* "Itchy coos" *to the* BABY.)

3RD WISE MAN   I also have brought a gift for the new born King.
       (*Orchestra stops*)
I have brought Myrrh.

MARY **JOSEPH** **OLLY** **SHEPHERDS** **OX and ASS**	What's that?

3RD WISE MAN   It's a transparent yellow-brown gum resin used as incense.

MARY **JOSEPH** **OLLY** **GABBY** **OX and ASS**	Pardon?

3RD WISE MAN **ANGY** **JELLY** **LOFTY**	It makes a nice smell!

(3RD WISE MAN *crosses to crib, lays down his gift. Greets* MARY *and* JOSEPH *and "Itchy coos" the* BABY.)

ASS   Hey! Angels! Hadn't you better get them to quieten down a bit. They're going to frighten the Baby at this rate.

OXY   Yeh! Get them to sing a lullaby to send him to sleep, or something. I could do with a bit of sleep myself. I'm shattered. And I've got to go to work tomorrow morning you know.

OLLY   Good thinking Oxy. A lullaby's the answer. Now are you ready?

Music No. 20. *LULLABY* (EVERYBODY).

(*4 bars intro.*)

ALL   Mummy loves you, yes, she does
        Daddy ,,   ,,   ,,   he ,,
        Olly   ,,   ,,   ,,   he ,,
        Gabby ,,   ,,   ,,   he ,,
        Lofty ,,   ,,   ,,   he ,,
        Jelly ,,   ,,   ,,   she ,,
        Angy   ,,   ,,   ,,   she ,,
        Oxy   ,,   ,,   ,,   he ,,
        Assy   ,,   ,,   ,,   he ,,
        We all love you, yes, we do.
        Sleep in heavenly peace.

OLLY	I like that! I'll tell you what, we'll get everyone to join in. (*Goes down to the footlights*) Now listen, you lot. I'll get everybody on stage started singing the song. And I'll come down. (*Calling*) And Gabby, you can come down as well, and then, you've just got to tell us what your first name is, and I'll get the Angels to sing it on stage. Right! I'll show you what I mean. All right, Angels. Get every-one lined up.
	(*Music No. 20 repeated, using names called out from Audience by* OLLY *and* GABBY.)
	(*Before song has ended,* HEROD *screams from back of auditorium.*)
HEROD	(*sings loudly*) HEROD LOVES ME, YES HE DOES. (*Speaks*) Where is the baby? I'm going to find him! Where is he? I'll find the little creepie and the "aagh!"
	(ANGEL CHICAGO *runs from back of auditorium calling* "Olly", *climbs onto stage.*)
CHICAGO	Olly! Where's Olly?
OLLY	I'm coming. (*Still in auditorium*) Here I am Chicago. What's the trouble?
CHICAGO	Olly! Herod's out of control. He means to find the baby and kill him, he doesn't want the new King to be allowed to live! He's getting ever so angry. I can't stop him any more. He wants to kill the baby!
OLLY	Hmm! We'll see about that! Jelly. Warn the Wise Men not to go back to Herod. He mustn't find out where the baby is.
JELLY	Yes Olly. (JELLY *crosses to* WISE MEN. *They are startled as he appears.*)
OLLY	Angy. Tell the shepherds to go back to their flocks and not to tell Herod's men where they've been.
ANGY	Yes Olly.
	(ANGY *goes offstage to tell* SHEPHERDS.)
OLLY	Lofty. Go and tell Mary and Joseph to prepare to run away with the baby.
LOFTY	Right Olly.

(LOFTY *crosses to* MARY *and* JOSEPH. *They react, then listen intently.*)

OLLY   Gabby. Keep a look out for Herod.

GABBY   Yes Olly.

OXY   Me too Olly!

ASSY   And me!

OLLY   (*still in auditorium*) O.K. Right. Angels, organize some clouds to hide Mary and Joseph.

(HEROD *heard screaming and shouting offstage left. Rant! Roar! etc.*)

GABBY   Olly, he's coming.

OXY   He's getting near Olly.

ASSY   He's searching all the houses! He's got some soldiers with him.

OLLY   Right. Hurry it up Angels. We haven't got all day.

(*Small wall of cloud is made to hide* MARY, JOSEPH *and crib.*)

Gabby! Chicago! Lofty! Get some cloud balls and bring them down here into the audience, and dish them out to everybody.

(HEROD *heard shouting offstage.*)

HEROD   (*off*) Rant! Roar! Have you found the baby yet?

OXY   Olly! Herod and the soldiers have stopped the three Wise Men in the street.

ASSY   They're asking them questions.

OXY   The three Wise Men are shaking their heads and pointing in the sky.

ASSY   They seem to be saying they've lost the star.

OXY   Herod and the soldiers have left them! They're coming this way!

HEROD   (*off*) Rant! Roar! I can smell the baby! Soldiers follow my nose!

(HEROD *shouting offstage. By now all angels are in auditorium giving cloud balls out.*)

OLLY	(*to audience*) Right! Pay attention. This is a very serious situation. We've got to keep absolutely quiet till the right moment. Can you all do that ? (*Wait for reaction*) Sshhh! Whisper. Can you all keep quiet? Good. Now I'll tell you when to throw. Shh! I think I can hear him coming.
	(HEROD *and* SOLDIERS *enter stage left with drawn swords.* HEROD *shushes the soldiers. If there's any noise* OLLY *shushes the audience. Crouched down,* HEROD *slowly crosses towards cloud hiding* MARY, JOSEPH *and* BABY. *On stage* OXY *and* ASSY *chew quicker and quicker—watching.* HEROD *pauses. Puts up his hands to stop soldiers.*)
HEROD	Shush! (*Listens*) I thought I heard something.
SOLDIERS	What!
OLLY	(*sotto voce*) Everybody keep quiet!
HEROD	No. I can't hear it now. But I can smell something. (*Sniffs loudly*) I can smell a baby! Soldiers forward. Over here somewhere. I can smell a fresher baby for us to kill. (*Heads towards wall of cloud at a slow creep.*)
OLLY	(*to audience*) Wait for it. Wait for it. Wait for it! (*As* HEROD *reaches cloud wall*) NOW!
	(ANGELS *and audience start throwing cloudballs at* HEROD *and* SOLDIERS. *More* ANGELS *appear from stage right, throwing cloudballs and blowing very hard.* OLLY, GABBY, JELLY, LOFTY *etc. come up from audience and join.*)
HEROD	(*retreating with soldiers*) I'm being stung by bits of grit or something. And this wind is terrible!
OLLY	Keep blowing!
HEROD	Come back soldiers! We must find the baby! Find something to hang on to!
	(*But all the soldiers but one have been blown into the wings. This one and* HEROD *have been bent by the wind until they stand making a perfect target for* OXY *and* ASSY—.)
	(OXY *and* ASSY *charge,* HEROD *and* SOLDIER *are butted into wings.*)
	(KING HEROD *re-enters.*)

HEROD (*shouting*) The weather's beaten me today, but I'll be back tomorrow!! I'll finally get all the babies!!!

(OXY *and* ASSY *charge again.* HEROD *runs offstage.* ANGELS *cheer* "*We've Won!*" *etc.*)

OLLY O.K. angels, Oxy and Assy. Let's have a bit of a clean up here. That's Herod's lot for today. He won't be back. Let's get rid of the clouds hiding Mary and Joseph. Has everyone thrown their cloud balls back.

(ANGELS *remove clouds.*)

(*to Audience*) Well done, everybody, you did very well there. Congratulations. Right. I'll just check that that's everything. (*Gets piece of paper out of pocket*) There's nothing worse when you go to the theatre than to get home and find they've missed a bit out. Now, let me see . . .

Music No. 21. "*KINDLY SIT DOWN*" — Reprise (OLLY).

OLLY (*Sings*) Now Mary and Joseph have had the baby,
Oxy and Assy have done their dance,
Even Gabby's a little bit taller
Because you nagged for a second chance.

The three Kings came and brought their pressies,
The Shepherds came and they sang a song.
Herod came and caused some trouble,
But we all made sure — he didn't stay long.

Angel Chicago was a little bit naughty
But he can't help it — I know that's true.
I think I'll give him a break from Herod
And let him be guardian to one of you.

(*Music continues under dialogue*)

(*spoken*) Would you like that? Would you? Who would like Angel Chicago as their Guardian Angel? One or two of you. Good.

GABBY Hey Olly!

(*Music stops*)

OLLY What?

GABBY	Well, Mary and Joseph still look a bit fed up. Shall I appear and tell them they're safe now?
OLLY	Certainly not. That's not allowed. But I'll tell you what we can do.
GABBY	What?
OLLY	Well, we can all make them feel happy.
GABBY	How?
OLLY	We get everyone to join in a happy song. Mary and Joseph won't be able to hear it—but they'll be able to sense it, and that'll make them happy, and they can set off on their journey with a smile.
GABBY	How do you mean?

(*Music No. 20 continues at letter D*) (*Under dialogue*)

OLLY	I'll show you. (*To Audience*) Now. Me and the Angels are going to start singing a song, and I want you to join in if you can and watch Mary and Joseph's face, and when they start to smile that means they can sense something nice happening—and then that means that they can set off on their journey—happy. Alright? O.K. Here's what we do. (*Direct segue*)

Music No. 22. "*CLAP YOUR HANDS AND BE CHEERY*" (OLLY *and* ENSEMBLE).

OLLY (*sings*)	Clap your hands and be cheery, Clap your hands and be cheery, Clap your hands and be cheery If you'll let him come in.
	Clap your hands and be cheery, Clap your hands and be cheery, Clap your hands and be cheery If you'll let him come in.
	There must be room! There must be room! Open your hearts And let him come in.

ENSEMBLE	Stamp your feet and be cheery Stamp your feet and be cheery Stamp your feet and be cheery If you'll let him come in.	**SOME SHOUTED** Clap your hands Clap your hands

56

ENSEMBLE (Cont'd.)	**SOME SHOUTED**
Stamp your feet and be cheery	Clap your hands
Stamp your feet and be cheery	Clap your hands
Stamp your feet and be cheery	
If you'll let him come in.	
There must be room!	
There must be room!	
Open your hearts	
And let him come in.	
Stand up and be cheery	Clap your hands
Stand up and be cheery	Stamp your feet
Stand up and be cheery	
If you'll let him come in.	
Stand up and be cheery	Clap your hands
Stand up and be cheery	Stamp your feet
Stand up and be cheery	
If you'll let him come in.	
There must be room!	
There must be room!	
Open your hearts	
And let him come in.	
Stand up and be cheery,	
Stand up and be cheery,	
Stand up and be cheery,	
If you'll let him come in!	

(1st Curtain)

Music No. 23. "*CLAP YOUR HANDS*"—Bows (ENSEMBLE).

(Orchestra play 24 bars during Bows, then)

ALL (*sing*)   Clap your hands and be cheery,
Clap your hands and be cheery,
Clap hands and be cheery
If you'll let him come in.

Clap your hands and be cheery,
Clap hands and be cheery,
Clap hands and be cheery
If you'll let him come in!

(Final Curtain)
Play-Out. Repeat No. 22 (Orchestra only) if desired.)

THE END